This young Native American boy is wearing ceremonial clothes for a gathering of groups of Plains Indians in Wyoming, U.S.A.

THE USBORNE BOOK OF
PEOPLES
OF THE
WORLD
INTERNET - LINKED

Gillian Doherty and Anna Claybourne

Designed by Laura Fearn and Linda Penny

Additional contributors: Nathalie Abi-Ezzi,
Kamini Khanduri and Rebecca Treays
Managing editor: Felicity Brooks
Managing designer: Stephen Wright
Cover design: Laura Fearn and Zöe Wray
Digital image processing: John Russell and Mike Olley
Picture research: Ruth King
Cartographic editors: Craig Asquith
and Christine Johnston

Consultants:
Professor Michael Hitchcock, University of North London
Dr. Uwem Ite, Department of Geography, University of Lancaster
Susan Bermingham, M.A, Head of Humanities,
Royton and Crompton School, Oldham
Dr. Stephanie Bunn, University of Manchester
Dr. Susan Pfisterer, Menzies Centre for Australian Studies,
King's College, University of London
Dr. Vivien Miller, Senior Lecturer in American Studies, Middlesex University
Dr. Francisco Dominguez, Head of Latin American Studies, Middlesex University
Dr. Elizabeth Bomberg, Department of Politics, University of Edinburgh
Dr. Simon Kirby, Department of Theoretical and Applied Linguistics,
University of Edinburgh

Children at a carnival in Guadeloupe, in the Caribbean

CONTENTS

ᚚᚚᚚ Internet links ᚚᚚᚚ

Throughout this book there are boxes like this one containing details of interesting, relevant Web sites. The best way to access these sites is to go to Usborne Quicklinks at **www.usborne-quicklinks.com**. There you will find links that you can click on to take you straight to the sites. We will regularly review and update the links, so you will always be able to access Usborne-recommended sites.

All the sites in this book have been carefully selected by Usborne editors. However, we are not responsible for the accuracy or suitability of the material on any Web site other than our own. We recommend that young children using the Internet are supervised by a parent or teacher. You will find general guidelines on using the Internet on page 92.

WORLD MAP

Severnaya Zemlya

New Siberia Islands

ARCTIC

OCEAN

Wrangel Island

Beaufort Sea

Victoria Island

Arctic Circle

Siberia

Alaska (U.S.A.)

RUSSIA ○ Yakutsk

Anchorage ○

Lena

Yukon

Yenisey

Bering Sea

Great Plains

C A N A

○ Ulan Bator

MONGOLIA

Aleutian Islands

Vancouver ○

Gobi Desert

Beijing (Peking) ○

○ Shenyang

N. KOREA

Seoul ○ **S. KOREA**

JAPAN ○ Tokyo

PACIFIC

San Francisco ○

UNITED STATE OF AMERICA

Chicag

CHINA

○ Tianjin

Osaka ○

○ Los Angeles

Plateau of Tibet

Chongqing ○

Yangtze

○ Shanghai

OCEAN

Midway Islands (U.S.A.)

Tropic of Cancer

Gulf Mex

NEPAL **BHUTAN**

Guangzhou (Canton) ○

TAIWAN

MEXICO

BANGLADESH

Dhaka ●

Hanoi ○

Hong Kong

Hawaiian Islands (U.S.A.)

Mexico City ○

MYANMAR (BURMA)

Yangon (Rangoon) ●

THAILAND

Bangkok ●

VIETNAM

Manila ○

Northern Mariana Islands (U.S.A.)

MARSHALL ISLANDS

BELI

GUATEMALA

SALVAD

CAMBODIA

South China Sea

PHILIPPINES

PALAU

FEDERATED STATES OF MICRONESIA

NAURU

Kuala Lumpur ○

MALAYSIA

Borneo

KIRIBATI

Equator

Galapagos Islands (Ecuador)

Putrajaya ●

SINGAPORE

Sumatra

INDONESIA

New Guinea

PAPUA NEW GUINEA

SOLOMON ISLANDS

TUVALU

Line Islands

International Date Line

Marquesas Islands

Jakarta ○

Java

EAST TIMOR

Darwin ○

Port Moresby ●

SAMOA

Society Islands

Tuamotu Archipelago

Pitcairn Islands (U.K.)

INDIAN

VANUATU

FIJI

FRENCH POLYNESIA

OCEAN

New Caledonia (France)

TONGA

Tropic of Capricorn

AUSTRALIA

Brisbane ○

Perth ○

Sydney ○

PACIFIC

Canberra ○

Melbourne ○

NEW ZEALAND

Wellington ○

OCEAN

Chatham Islands (New Zealand)

Antarctic Circle

Ross Sea

A N T A R

4

GREENLAND
(Denmark)

Ellesmere
Island

Baffin
Bay

Baffin
Island

Labrador

Newfoundland

Nuuk
(Godthåb)

ICELAND

Reykjavik

Faroe Islands
(Denmark)

North Cape

Svalbard
(Norway)

Franz Josef Land

Severnaya
Zemlya

Novaya
Zemlya

N O R W A Y

S W E D E N

Lapland

FINLAND

Oslo

Helsinki

Stockholm

St. Petersburg

ESTONIA

DENMARK

LATVIA

LITHUANIA

Moscow

R U S S I A

Ural Mountains

Ob

Yenisey

Astana

K A Z A K S T A N

UNITED
KINGDOM

Dublin

IRELAND

London

NETHERLANDS

Paris

FRANCE

GERMANY

CZ. REP.

SWITZ.

Warsaw

POLAND

BELARUS

Kiev

UKRAINE

SLOVAKIA

AUSTRIA HUNGARY

SLOV.

MOLDOVA

ROMANIA

Montréal

Ottawa

New York

Washington D.C.

ATLANTIC

OCEAN

Bermuda
(U.K.)

Azores
(Portugal)

Madeira
(Portugal)

PORTUGAL

Lisbon

Madrid

SPAIN

Algiers

Rome

ITALY

BOS. &
HERZ.

CRO.

YUGO.

ALB.

MAC.

BULGARIA

Athens

GREECE

Tunis

Black Sea

Istanbul

Ankara

T U R K E Y

GEORGIA

ARMENIA AZERBAIJAN

Caspian
Sea

Aral
Sea

UZBEKISTAN

TURKMENISTAN

Tashkent

KYRGYZSTAN

TAJIKISTAN

C H I N A

Volga

Danube

MAURITANIA

Rabat

MOROCCO

Atlas Mountains

Laâyoune

WESTERN
SAHARA

Canary Islands
(Spain)

TUNISIA

Tripoli

Cairo

ALGERIA

LIBYA

EGYPT

Sahara Desert

Mediterranean Sea

CYPRUS

SYRIA

LEBANON

ISRAEL

JORDAN

IRAQ

Baghdad

KUWAIT

I R A N

Tehran

Ashgabat

Kabul

AFGHANISTAN

Islamabad

Himalaya Mountains

Plateau of
Tibet

NEPAL

New
Delhi

Delhi

BHUTAN

BANGLADESH

Dhaka

Ganges

ssau

BAHAMAS

CUBA

DOMINICAN
REPUBLIC

HAITI

JAMAICA

Santo Domingo

ONDURAS

CA

STA

PANAMA

CARAGUA

Caribbean
Sea

Caracas

VENEZUELA

Bogotá

COLOMBIA

uito

ECUADOR

PERU

Lima

Amazon

CAPE VERDE

Nouakchott

Dakar

SENEGAL

MALI

Bamako

GUINEA

SIERRA
LEONE

LIBERIA

IVORY
COAST

GHANA

NIGER

Niamey

BURKINA
FASO

NIGERIA

Abuja

Lagos

Yaoundé

CAMEROON

Libreville

GABON

CONGO

Brazzaville

CHAD

N'Djamena

SUDAN

Khartoum

CENTRAL AFRICAN
REPUBLIC

Bangui

DEMOCRATIC
REPUBLIC OF
CONGO

Kinshasa

Luanda

ANGOLA

Congo

ERITREA

Asmara

Sana

YEMEN

Addis Ababa

ETHIOPIA

UGANDA

Kampala

Lake
Victoria

KENYA

Nairobi

SOMALIA

Mogadishu

Dodoma

TANZANIA

Red Sea

SAUDI
ARABIA

Riyadh

UNITED
ARAB
EMIRATES

OMAN

Muscat

Arabian
Sea

Karachi

PAKISTAN

I N D I A

Mumbai
(Bombay)

Kolkata
(Calcutta)

Bay
of Bengal

MYANMAR
(BURMA)

Yangon
(Rangoon)

THAILAND

Colombo

SRI LANKA

MALDIVES

SEYCHELLES

COMOROS

MALAWI

MADAGASCAR

Antananarivo

MAURITIUS

Réunion
(France)

I N D I A N

O C E A N

BRAZIL

La Paz

BOLIVIA

Sucre

PARAGUAY

São Paulo

Brasília

Rio de Janeiro

Asunción

URUGUAY

Montevideo

Santiago

CHILE

ARGENTINA

Buenos
Aires

Ascension
(U.K.)

St. Helena
(U.K.)

ATLANTIC

OCEAN

NAMIBIA

Windhoek

BOTSWANA

Gaborone

ZAMBIA

Lusaka

Harare

ZIMBABWE

MOZAMBIQUE

SWAZILAND

Pretoria

Maputo

SOUTH
AFRICA

LESOTHO

Cape Town

Cape of Good Hope

Kerguélen
(France)

Falkland Islands
(U.K.)

South Georgia
(U.K.)

South
Sandwich
Islands
(U.K.)

Cape Horn

Antarctic
Peninsula

C T I C A

WHAT ARE PEOPLE?

This book is about people and our different lifestyles, languages, religions and cultures. Humans have the most advanced culture of any species. But what are humans, and what makes us different from other animals?

A young child learns language by listening to people talk and copying them. Gradually children learn to make up their own new sentences.

The human species

Human beings are just one of millions of different kinds, or species, of animals that live on Earth. We belong to a group of animals called primates, which includes apes and monkeys. However, the way we behave is very different from all other types of animals. Humans have unusually large, complicated brains. We try to question why things happen and where we came from, and look for ways to show how we feel. This is why we are the only animals to have science and religion. We also have a complex culture, which means things like art, music, clothes and customs.

These animals are bonobos, a type of ape. They share many similarities with humans, but they are still very different from us in the way they look and behave.

Language

Humans have a much more advanced use of language than other animals. With language, we can explain ideas to each other, store information in books and computers, and pass on our knowledge to future generations.

The earliest known writing was used by the Sumerians, who lived about 5,000 years ago. Now there are hundreds of different alphabets and writing styles, which are known as scripts.

▷▷	mountain
⊞⊐	head
▷	food
⊗⊗	water
▷⊠⊁	bird
⊀	fish
▷⊳	ox

This Sumerian writing, called cuneiform, is one of the oldest writing systems in the world.

This woman is wearing court dress to perform a traditional Japanese tea ceremony.

Ethnic groups

This book often uses the terms "ethnic groups" and "peoples" to describe groups of people who live together, or who see themselves as a group. Ethnic groups can be large or small. They can live together or be spread over a wide area. But the people who belong to an ethnic group usually have several things in common. They may share the same language, culture or religion.

Groups of people

People are social animals. This means we like to live in groups and communicate with each other. The simplest human group is the family, a group of people linked together by birth, adoption or fostering. People also form other groups, such as bands, teams, towns, cities, political parties and whole countries.

These are dancers from Congo, in Africa, wearing costumes made from grasses. People often wear costumes or uniforms to show that they belong to a particular group.

Types of people

Wherever you go, there are differences between people. Some are taller than others. Some can run faster than others. There are people of different sexes, ages and abilities. Some people are very good at learning facts, others might be good at sports or cooking.

Sometimes, differences in appearance can help you recognize where a person might be from. But people have been moving around, or migrating, for thousands of years, so most countries have many different types of people living in them.

PEOPLES AND CULTURE

C ulture means "way of life". The culture of a society or group of people includes their customs, hobbies, foods, fashions, beliefs and ways of celebrating things. Your culture depends on things like your family background, the country you live in, and your age.

Fashions, such as the clothes worn by these Japanese girls, can change very quickly.

Types of culture

Popular culture includes everyday leisure activities, fashions and media (such as TV and magazines). This type of culture changes quickly, but traditional culture is also important to most people. Religious rituals, birthday songs, and foods eaten on particular days are examples of traditional culture that stay the same from one generation to the next.

Many parts of the world, especially big cities, are multicultural. This means that they have people with many different cultures living in them. Multicultural societies often arise when groups of people migrate from one place to live in another, taking their culture with them.

Religion

Most people in the world are religious. This means they have a set of spiritual beliefs about why the world exists and what happens after death. The main religions are Buddhism, Christianity, Hinduism, Islam (whose followers are called Muslims), Judaism (whose followers are called Jews) and Sikhism.

Muslims, Christians, Jews and Sikhs believe in just one god. Hindus have many gods, who are all part of an overriding force called Brahman. Buddhism does not focus on gods, but involves following a set of rules in order to achieve a state called nirvana.

This woman from Bali, in Indonesia, is praying. Most religious people speak to their gods or spirits by praying.

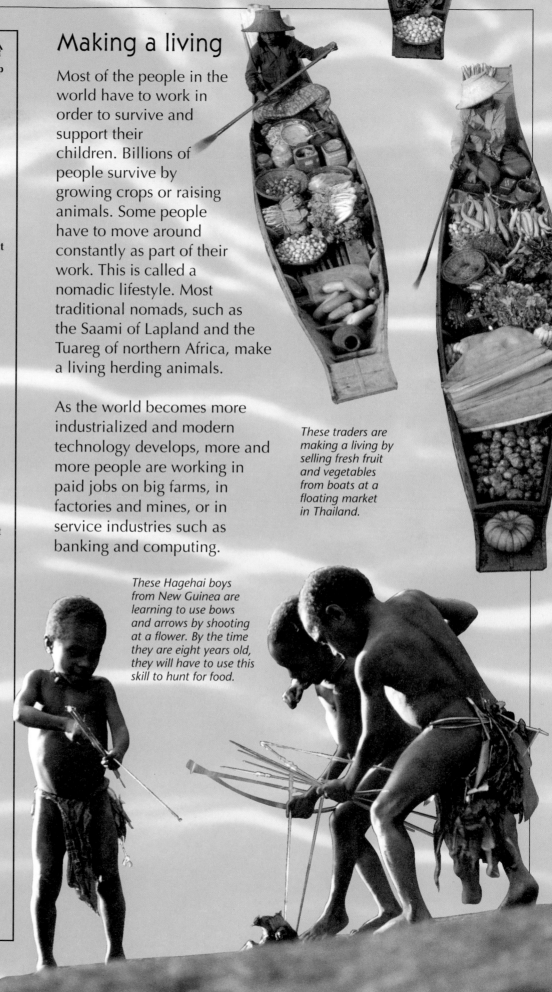

Internet links 👪 👪

Here are some useful Web sites to help you find out about different peoples and their cultures:

General

This Web site has detailed, up-to-date fact files on all the world's countries:
www.odci.gov/cia/publications/factbook/index.html

See how quickly the world's population is changing on this population clock:
metalab.unc.edu/lunarbin/worldpop

On this Web site you can find out what the time is anywhere in the world:
www.worldtimeserver.com

Here you can calculate currency conversions at the touch of a button:
www.xe.net/ucc/full.shtml

Languages

On this Web site you can find out which languages are most widely spoken and which are in danger:
www.linguasphere.org/

This site has dictionaries and online translators for many different languages:
rivendel.com/~ric/resources/inter.html

Did you know that your gestures may mean different things in different cultures? Find out more on this site:
www.webofculture.com/refs/gestures.html

Here you can see examples of different writing systems:
logos.uoregon.edu/explore/orthography

Food around the world

Try out delicious recipes from different countries:
library.thinkquest.org/3195

Read about insect snacks that people around the world eat:
www.uky.edu/Agriculture/Entomology/ythfacts/bugfood/yf813.htm

Find out about street food eaten in different parts of the world:
www.openair.org/opair/strtfood.html

Religions and festivals

Learn about some of the main religions of the world on this Web site:
www.ipl.org/cgi-bin/youth/youth.out.pl?sub=owd1000

Discover how people celebrate New Year's Eve in different countries:
riceinfo.rice.edu/projects/topics/internatl/holidays/new-years-page1.htm

For quick and easy access to these sites go to
www.usborne-quicklinks.com

Making a living

Most of the people in the world have to work in order to survive and support their children. Billions of people survive by growing crops or raising animals. Some people have to move around constantly as part of their work. This is called a nomadic lifestyle. Most traditional nomads, such as the Saami of Lapland and the Tuareg of northern Africa, make a living herding animals.

As the world becomes more industrialized and modern technology develops, more and more people are working in paid jobs on big farms, in factories and mines, or in service industries such as banking and computing.

These traders are making a living by selling fresh fruit and vegetables from boats at a floating market in Thailand.

These Hagehai boys from New Guinea are learning to use bows and arrows by shooting at a flower. By the time they are eight years old, they will have to use this skill to hunt for food.

American football fans wave pom-poms at the Rose Bowl stadium, Los Angeles, California

NORTH AMERICA

NORTH AMERICA

The name "North America" is sometimes confusing, as it can be used to mean several different things. In this book, the northern part of the American continent begins with Panama in the south and stretches up to Canada and Greenland in the north. It includes the U.S.A., Mexico, Central America and the Caribbean.

This map shows where North America is.

Different lands

The landscape and climate of North America is extremely varied. Greenland and Alaska in the far north are cold, icy and sparsely populated, Arizona in the U.S.A. has vast stretches of desert, and Central America is dominated by hot, humid rainforests. Cities such as New York and Mexico City are among the biggest in the world and are filled with towering skyscrapers.

This dancer is a member of the Blackfeet group of Native Americans. He is performing at a special meeting called a powwow.

Native Americans

Native Americans are the people who lived in North America before European explorers arrived. Each Native American group had its own lifestyles and customs and was governed by a chief.

In the 19th century, the European settlers forced Native Americans to live on areas of land called reservations. They tried to force them to speak English, wear European clothes and become Christians. As a result, many Native American languages and traditions were forgotten. Now languages are being revived and Native Americans make and sell traditional pottery, baskets or textiles. Some groups also run casinos on their reservations.

Living in America

North America is home to some of the world's richest and poorest countries. The wealthy U.S.A. (often known simply as America) is one of the world's most powerful nations, while Guatemala has been bankrupted by years of war and is extremely poor.

👥 Internet links 👥

Here you can play a Native American game and try some quizzes:
www.bluemountain.com/eng/nativeamer/NativeAmer.html
Here you can find out about different Native American communities:
www.germantown.k12.il.us/html/intro.html

For quick and easy access to these sites go to
www.usborne-quicklinks.com

Alaska, in the far north of the continent, is one of the 50 states of the U.S.A.

Central America is the long strip of land from Guatemala to Panama that joins Mexico to South America.

This chain of islands reaching across the Caribbean Sea is usually known as the West Indies or the Caribbean.

The city of Las Vegas in the southwest of the U.S.A. is known for its bright lights and entertainment industry.

Point Barrow
Aleutian Islands
GREENLAND (Denmark)
Ellesmere Island
Arctic Circle
Alaska (U.S.A.)
Anchorage
Yukon
Victoria Island
Baffin Island
Nuuk (Godthåb)
Cape Farewell
Mackenzie
Juneau
CANADA
Labrador
Vancouver Island
Vancouver
Seattle
Portland
Edmonton
Calgary
Winnipeg
Newfoundland
Columbia
Rocky Mountains
Great Plains
Missouri
Great Lakes
Québec
Ottawa
Montréal
St. Lawrence
San Francisco
Salt Lake City
UNITED STATES
Denver
Minneapolis
Toronto
Detroit
Chicago
Boston
New York
Las Vegas
Los Angeles
San Diego
Colorado
Phoenix
OF AMERICA
Kansas City
Ohio
Appalachian Mts.
Philadelphia
Washington D.C.
Dallas
Mississippi
Atlanta
Cape Hatteras
Bermuda (U.K.)
Tropic of Cancer
Rio Grande
Houston
Monterrey
Tampa
Miami
Nassau
THE BAHAMAS
Tropic of Cancer
MEXICO
Havana
CUBA
Puerto Rico (U.S.A.)
ANTIGUA & BARBUDA
Mexico City
Yucatán Peninsula
DOMINICAN REPUBLIC
HAITI
Port-au-Prince
JAMAICA
Santo Domingo
ST. KITTS & NEVIS
DOMINICA
Guadeloupe (France)
Martinique (France)
Sierra Madre
Acapulco
BELIZE
GUATEMALA
ST. LUCIA
ST. VINCENT & THE GRENADINES
BARBADOS
Guatemala City
HONDURAS
EL SALVADOR
Tegucigalpa
GRENADA
TRINIDAD & TOBAGO
San Salvador
Managua
NICARAGUA
Port of Spain
COSTA RICA
San José
Panamá
PANAMA

THE U.S.A.

The United States of America, also known as the U.S.A. or America, is a huge country, although it's not much more than half the size of Russia, the biggest country. The U.S.A. is very rich and has immense political and cultural influence worldwide.

The U.S.A. has hundreds of large theme parks with huge rides like this roller coaster.

Land and law

The U.S.A. is divided into 50 states. Power is shared between state governments and a central federal government based in the capital, Washington D.C. The southern states are warm, green and rich in oil, while the main farming areas are in the western states. The northeast is the main business region. Manufacturing has moved more to the southern states in recent years. Many computer companies are located in Silicon Valley in California.

Dr. Martin Luther King Jr., the leader of the 1960s Civil Rights movement for equality for black Americans, speaks at a "March against Fear" rally in 1966.

The 'American Dream'

People from all over the world have moved to the U.S.A., and a million new immigrants arrive each year. Many are following the 'American Dream': the belief that, in America, anyone can become rich and successful. However, many Americans are still very poor.

The crowned figure in the background is the Statue of Liberty in New York. It is a symbol of the political freedom enshrined in the Constitution of the U.S.A.

The mixture of peoples gives the U.S.A. a rich, diverse culture. Jazz and blues music, for instance, developed out of rhythms brought to the U.S.A. from Africa, while cheesecake and bagels were originally Jewish foods.

🚶 Internet links 🚶

Here you can see video clips and hear songs from America's past:
www.americaslibrary.gov/cgi-bin/page.cgi/sh
On this Web site you can find out how Americans celebrate the anniversary of their independence:
www.usacitylink.com/usa
On this Web site you can find out about the structure of the government of the U.S.A.:
pittsford.monroe.edu/Schools/Jefferson/GOVERNMENT/GovFrame.html

For quick and easy access to these sites go to **www.usborne-quicklinks.com**

Entertainment

Entertainment is big business in the U.S.A. The country's main movie-making area, Hollywood, in California, produces films that can cost many millions of dollars to make, but which earn even more. Theme parks are also very popular.

Science and power

The U.S.A. is the leading political world power, and science and technology have played an important part in its success. Nuclear science, which can be used to make powerful bombs, has helped give the U.S.A. political strength. As a result, the U.S.A. now plays a big part in making wars and keeping peace around the world. The nation's wealth and success also owe a lot to computer science, and the U.S.A. dominates Internet technology. American English is the main language of the Internet.

Minnie Mouse posing for a photo with a young boy in Disney World, a theme park based on famous characters from the cartoons of Walt Disney

The reusable Space Shuttle spacecraft is part of America's world-famous multi-billion dollar space exploration industry.

THE FAR NORTH

In Canada, people ski in resorts where there are ski lifts and other facilities, but people also ski cross country just to get from place to place.

The far north of North America is taken up by Greenland, Canada and Alaska (part of the U.S.A.). This is a vast area: Canada is the second largest country in the world, and Greenland is the world's biggest island.

Many cultures

Canada is divided into ten provinces and three territories: the Yukon, Nunavut and the Northwest Territories.

Many Canadians have British, French or Native American ancestors and the offical languages are English and French. French culture is strong in the province of Québec where cafes and shops reflect its influence.

Skiers swoop down a slope at the Lake Louise Ski Area in Banff National Park, Alberta, Canada. Many tourists visit Canada for its natural beauty and outdoor activities.

Natural resources

Most Canadians live in large cities along the border with the U.S.A. The rest of the country has a varied landscape, including lakes, mountains, forests and grasslands, or prairies. These provide rich natural resources such as timber, water, gas, oil and minerals. Outside the cities, many people's jobs are based around mining and forestry.

Winter sports

Outdoor sports and activities such as canoeing, riding horses and rafting are popular in Canada. But the country is particularly known for its winter sports, especially ice hockey which can be played on frozen ponds and lakes.

Snowmobiling at a winter sports festival in Canada

Greenland

Although Greenland is the world's largest island, its population is very small because conditions there are so harsh. Most of Greenland lies within the Arctic Circle, and its central region is covered by a layer of ice that never melts.

The island has a small road network, but planes and dog sleds provide a flexible and reliable way of getting around. The majority of Greenlanders live along the coast, where the climate is mildest, making a living from catching fish, shrimps and seals.

Who are the Inuit?

The Inuit are the native people of northern Canada. In 1999, the Canadian government made part of the Northwest Territories into a new Inuit territory, giving back land which the Inuit had lost to settlers. The new territory is called Nunavut, which means "our land" in Inukitut, the Inuit language.

The Inuit keep their traditions alive by speaking Inukitut, hunting for food, and making wood and bone carvings. They also take advantage of modern technology, using snowmobiles, telephones and computers.

👪 Internet links 👪

Why not take a virtual trip around Nunavut and learn the Inuit language?
www.arctictravel.com
Explore Canada from space and discover its varied landscape for yourself:
www.ccrs.nrcan.gc.ca/ccrs/imgserv/tour/toure.html

For quick and easy access to these sites go to
www.usborne-quicklinks.com

Villages in Greenland are small. This one has about 500 human residents and 2,000 sled dogs, which are used for hunting and transportation.

These Inuit people are wearing heavy animal-skin coats to keep warm.

MEXICO

Mexico is a big country between the U.S.A. and Central America. It is very mountainous, but most Mexicans live in towns and cities in the middle of the country, where the land is flat.

A reconstruction of the Aztec calendar, on display in the National Museum of Anthropology in Mexico City

The Aztecs

From the mid-14th century, Mexico was ruled by the Aztecs, a Native American people. They built an empire with a capital city called Tenochtitlan and ruled over many Native American peoples. The empire ended when the Spanish conquered Mexico in 1519. Today's Mexicans are mainly *mestizos*, of mixed Spanish and Native American descent.

Hot and spicy

Mexican food is popular all over the world. *Guacamole* (mashed avocados), *tortillas* (flat bread), and meat and beans cooked in tomato sauce with hot chillies* are typical Mexican dishes. Over 60 different kinds of chillies are grown in Mexico. In some areas, people eat salads made out of cactus plants.

Corn tortilla chips are eaten with Mexican-style dips around the world.

Mexico City

Mexico City, the capital of Mexico, was built directly over the ruins of the Aztec capital. Today it is the world's biggest city, with 22 million people. The majority of the country's business is there, and the city is extremely busy, with lots of noise and traffic. It lies in a valley overlooked by volcanoes, and is regularly affected by earthquakes. The soil beneath it is so soft and swampy that the city sinks a little each year.

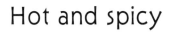

Tomatoes, chillies and beans are key ingredients in many Mexican dishes.*

*Chilies (U.S.A.)

Day of the Dead

The Day of the Dead is a joyous celebration that takes place on November 2 each year. All over Mexico, markets and shops sell skeletons and skulls made out of sugar or bread. People also dress up as skeletons and dance in huge parades. At home, families make small altars which they use to pray for and remember their dead friends and relatives. They decorate the altars with flowers, candles, food and photographs of those they want to remember.

👪 Internet links 👪

Here you can see what items traditionally make up altars for the Day of the Dead and find out how to bake the "bread of the dead":
www.azcentral.com/rep/dead
This Web site looks at the religion, culture and everyday life of the Aztecs:
library.thinkquest.org/27981

For quick and easy access to these sites go to
www.usborne-quicklinks.com

This skeleton model has been made from papier-mâché for a Day of the Dead parade.

CENTRAL AMERICA

These girls are dressed as angels to take part in a religious procession in El Salvador. Religious festivals are common in Central America.

Central America is the narrow strip of land, or isthmus, connecting North and South America. The landscape of Central America is mainly made up of mountains and volcanoes and people's lives are affected by frequent earthquakes and volcanic eruptions.

Takeover

Like Mexico, Central America was conquered by the Spanish 500 years ago, and many people living there today are of mixed Spanish and Native American descent. But each country has its own mix of peoples. As well as Native Americans and people of European descent, there are people of African descent along the Caribbean coast.

Land of the Maya

The Maya had a powerful empire around AD200-900, when they built great cities. Their empire covered most of Guatemala, and parts of Belize, Mexico, Honduras and El Salvador. Ruined cities can still be found in the jungles of Guatemala. The Maya are no longer powerful, but they still make up nearly half of Guatemala's population.

This Mayan girl in Guatemala is carrying a younger child on her back, wrapped in a traditional Mayan shawl.

👪 Internet links 👪

Discover how to make worry dolls using toothpicks and thread on this Web site: tqjunior.thinkquest.org/5737/worrydolls.html

Embark on a Mayan adventure, looking at ancient sites and carrying out experiments. There's a log book to record your journey: www.sci.mus.mn.us/sln/ma/map.html

For quick and easy access to these sites go to www.usborne-quicklinks.com

The Soccer War

Central America has suffered from decades of civil wars and conflict between countries. One war broke out between El Salvador and Honduras in 1969, after they had played soccer against each other in the World Cup. The real reasons, however, were disagreements over land, trade, and Salvadorean refugees in Honduras.

Worry dolls

Children in Central America sometimes make tiny, bright dolls called worry dolls. There is a legend that if they tell the dolls their worries at night and then place them under their pillows, by morning all their worries will have disappeared.

These tiny dolls are worry dolls. Their clothes are made by wrapping thread around the bodies.

The Panama Canal

The Panama Canal is one of the most important waterways in the world. It is a channel of water 80km (50 miles) long that cuts through Panama, linking the Atlantic Ocean with the Pacific Ocean. Each vessel that uses the canal must pay a fee according to its weight. This means that while ships pay thousands of dollars, Richard Halliburton, who swam through the canal in 1928, only paid 36 cents.

A thatched bohio, or hut, in a rainforest clearing in Panama. Huts like these are the homes of the Guaymi people, who live on the border between Panama and Costa Rica.

Rainforest life

A large area of Central America is covered by rainforest, which is home to a huge variety of plants and animals. But the rainforest is being devastated and many plants and animals may die out as trees are cut down to make timber for export, and to clear land for farming.

THE CARIBBEAN

A rich variety of fruit is grown on the tropical islands of the Caribbean.

Pineapple

T he Caribbean is the name given to the chain of hundreds of tropical islands stretching from North America to South America across the Caribbean Sea.

Slavery

From around 1500, Europeans fought with each other over possession of the Caribbean islands. They brought slaves from Africa, the Middle East, the Far East, and India to work on sugar, tobacco and cocoa plantations. Many of today's inhabitants are descendants of these slaves. Languages from around the world have combined to form unique regional dialects known as *creoles*.

Mango

Papaya

Plantains are green fruits which belong to the same family as bananas.

Tourism

The Caribbean islands are known for their white sandy beaches, clear blue sea and tropical sunshine. Their beauty and isolation has given them a reputation of being a "paradise on earth". As a result, tourism is one of the Caribbean's most important industries.

Tourists often go diving in the clear blue sea of the Caribbean. This boy is looking at a shell he has found while diving at Virgin Gorda, in the British Virgin Islands.

Hard work

Although the Caribbean may be seen as a paradise by people who go there as tourists, life is not always easy for its inhabitants. Many of those who do not work in the tourist industry make a living growing sugar cane, the Caribbean's main export, and other crops such as bananas, coffee and tobacco. Some of the poorest states, such as Haiti, suffer from severe unemployment. Many Haitians have to cross the border into the wealthier Dominican Republic to find work.

Music

Africa has had an important influence on the music of the Caribbean. Many Caribbean musical styles, such as reggae, conga, cha-cha-cha, plena and calypso, have African roots. Calypso, which originated in Trinidad is the music style most associated with the Caribbean. Calypso songs are often improvised and tend to focus on social and political subjects.

Street parties

Carnivals held to mark religious festivals are an important part of island life. The main carnival season takes place before Lent (the period of 40 days leading up to Easter in the Christian calendar). The streets are filled with parades, loud music, and people singing and dancing in bright costumes.

Junkanoo is a huge festival in the Bahamas. People make flamboyant costumes like this to take part in parades.

👪 Internet links 👪

Here you can read snippets of information about the different Caribbean islands:
www.geographia.com/indx02.htm

For quick and easy access to this site go to
www.usborne-quicklinks.com

A busy outdoor market in Zumbahua, Ecuador

SOUTH AMERICA

SOUTH AMERICA

The people of South America have a huge range of cultures and backgrounds. Over the centuries, waves of settlers have arrived from Europe, Africa and Asia to join the Native Americans who have lived there for thousands of years.

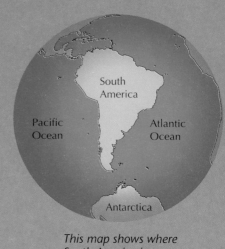

This map shows where South America is.

Empty and crowded

Much of South America is covered in rainforest, mountains and deserts where it can be hard to survive. Many people live in small villages and most work as farmers. Yet the coast has some of the world's biggest cities, with towering skyscrapers and crowded shanty towns.

Caracas
VENEZUELA
Medellín
Bogotá
Cali
COLOMBIA
Orinoco
Guiana Highlands
Georgetown
Paramaribo
Cayenne
GUYANA
SURINAME
FRENCH GUIANA

Equator
Equator

Galapagos Islands (Ecuador)
Quito
ECUADOR

Belém
Fortaleza

Amazon
Manaus

S e l v a s

B R A Z I L

Recife

PERU
Lima

M a t o
G r o s s o

São Francisco

Salvador

Brasília

Brazilian Highlands

Lake Titicaca
La Paz
BOLIVIA
Sucre

Belo Horizonte

Atacama Desert

PARAGUAY

Rio de Janeiro
São Paulo
Tropic of Capricorn
Curitiba

Asunción

Paraná

Porto Alegre

A n d e s

Córdoba
Rosario
URUGUAY

Santiago

Pampas

Buenos Aires
Montevideo

C H I L E

A R G E N T I N A
A n d e s

Patagonia

Falkland Islands (U.K.)

Tierra del Fuego

Cape Horn

Native Americans

Experts think the first South Americans came from Asia. They probably walked across a narrow strip of land in the far north, which once joined what are now Russia and Alaska. Their descendents now live mostly in South America's mountainous countries, such as Colombia, Bolivia, Ecuador and Peru.

Catholic continent

Although there are many different types of people in South America, over 90% of them are Roman Catholics. This form of Christianity was introduced by Spanish and Portuguese invaders who took control of the continent in the 1500s. There are now Catholic churches and statues all over South America, and many Christian festivals are celebrated.

Other religions

Many South Americans worship traditional Native American or African gods and spirits, often as well as attending a Catholic church. Some of the traditional religions have priests called shamans, who are believed to have magical powers.

Latin languages

South America is sometimes called Latin America, because most South Americans speak the Latin-based languages Spanish and Portuguese. These were brought by European invaders in the 16th century. However, many people speak Native American languages, such as Quechua and Aymara.

This crowded beach is the famous Copacabana beach in Rio de Janeiro, Brazil.

👫👫 Internet links 👫👫

On this site you can learn to weave with the descendants of the Incas:
www.incas.org
Here you can listen to haunting songs from the heart of the Andes and take a basic Quechua lesson:
www.andes.org

For quick and easy access to these sites go to
www.usborne-quicklinks.com

A shaman collects bark from a rainforest tree to use in traditional medicines.

IN THE MOUNTAINS

The vast Andes mountain range snakes down the western side of South America, through Colombia, Ecuador, Peru, Bolivia, Chile and Argentina. Despite dangers from volcanoes and earthquakes, the Andes are home to millions of miners, farmers, craftspeople and city-dwellers.

This young boy from Ecuador is harnessing a llama to lead it to market.

Fertile farms

The peaks of the Andes are covered in snow, but the lower slopes are good for growing crops. Mountain farmers grow corn, coffee and other crops on small plots of land, sometimes with terraces to stop the soil from being washed away. If the land is not good enough for crops, they keep herds of mountain animals, such as llamas and alpacas, which provide milk and wool, and which may also be used to transport goods.

Craft work

Many Native Americans live in villages in the Andes. Some earn a living from traditional crafts. They weave brightly striped shawls, blankets and hats. These are used by local people as well as being sold to tourists and exported around the world.

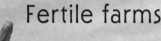

A traditional mountain folk band playing for tourists in Machu Picchu, Peru

Mountain music

The traditional folk music of the Andes combines Native American and Spanish sounds. It is usually played outside in the street or at folk clubs called *peñas*. When musicians play for tourists, they often wear traditional dress.

This is a view over La Paz, Bolivia. At over 3,650m (12,000ft), it is the world's highest capital city.

Cities

The Andes has some large cities, including Colombia's capital, Bogotá, and La Paz, one of Bolivia's two capitals (the other is Sucre). Most city-dwellers work in factories or mines. In the mountains there are huge deposits of gold, copper, tin, coal and jewels, especially emeralds. The biggest emerald mines are in Muzo, Colombia. While mine workers use modern machinery to extract the emeralds, poor *Guaqueros* (or "treasure hunters") sift through the dust and rubble, hoping to find leftover gems.

Inca influence

The Tahuantinsuyo, also known as the Incas, once ruled a large area of western South America. Their reign ended 400 years ago, but they still influence the Andean countries today.

Quechua, the Inca language, is spoken by about 13 million people. Mountain farmers use terraces that were built by the Incas, and ruined Inca cities, such as Machu Picchu in Peru, are tourist attractions.

This Peruvian girl in traditional costume is one of the Quechua people, who are descended from the Incas.

RAINFOREST PEOPLES

South America's huge Amazon valley is covered in millions of square miles of thick, humid rainforest. The Amazon rainforest is so big that it contains over a third of the world's trees. For thousands of years, it has also been the home of Native American peoples.

Leaders of the Kayapo people of Brazil sometimes wear lip-plates like these which emphasise their roles as public speakers.

Traditional lives

The rainforest is so vast that groups of people living in it have been cut off from the rest of the world for centuries. Some have only recently been discovered by outsiders. There may be others who have never had contact with the outside world. Rainforest peoples such as the Jivaro, Txikao and Kayapo have their own languages and customs. But many of them share similar lifestyles, surviving by hunting animals, gathering fruits and nuts, and growing crops in forest clearings.

Losing lifestyles

As new roads are built into the rainforest, the people who live there have more contact with outsiders. They may even lose their homes when parts of the rainforest are cut down. To make a living, they may have to learn more widely spoken languages or move away from the forest into towns and cities, leaving their old traditions and lifestyles behind.

🏃 Internet links 🏃

Here you can find out about the unique lifestyles of some of the peoples of the Venezuelan Amazon:
www.orinoco.org

Play a game where you try to run an ecotourism project in the Amazon:
www.eduweb.com/amazon.html

For quick and easy access to these sites go to
www.usborne-quicklinks.com

This man playing a wooden flute is one of the Jivaro people of the Amazon.

Clearing the forest

Rainforest trees provide all kinds of useful products, such as brazil nuts, cashew nuts, wax and rubber. At one time these things were simply collected from the forest, but now they are mostly farmed on plantations.

Traditionally, rainforest peoples cleared small areas of land to grow crops, and moved on after a few years. Because the cleared areas were tiny, this method, called shifting agriculture, did not harm much of the forest, and the trees eventually grew back. But since the 1960s, more rainforest has been cut down, for timber and to make space for farms, mines and factories. So the amount of rainforest is decreasing.

These are rainforest plants in Ecuador. Many rainforest plants can be used to make medicines.

Forest food

Although most rainforest peoples grow crops, they can also find food in the forest. Hunting and fishing provide them with a wide range of meat, including monkeys, toucans and caimans, which are reptiles similar to alligators. The Piaroa people of Venezuela sometimes eat tarantulas (a type of spider), cooking them by squeezing their insides onto a leaf and baking it over a fire.

Many rainforest peoples grow just enough food to supply their village. This woman is processing locally-grown manioc (a plant a little like a potato) to make flour.

COMBINED CULTURES

South American culture is influenced by the traditions of the different types of people who live there. For example, many South Americans love soccer, which came from Europe; samba music from Africa; and foods that combine Spanish, African and Native American influences.

Party!

Carnivals and costume parades take place frequently all over South America. Most of them celebrate Christian festivals, such as Lent, Easter and Christmas. They are lively occasions, with plenty of loud music, dancing, dressing up, eating and drinking. Many cities, towns and villages also hold their own local religious or historical celebrations.

Delicious dishes

All kinds of foods are eaten in South America. Argentinians and Uruguayans eat lots of meat, and Bolivians have dozens of varieties of potatoes. A typical meal in the Andes consists of fried beef, beans, a fried egg, rice and a slice of avocado. This type of dish is called *churrasco* in Ecuador and *bandeja paisa* in Colombia. Local delicacies include *cuy* (guinea pig) and *hormiga culona* (fried ants) in Colombia, and iguana (a type of lizard) in Guyana.

This Peruvian woman is preparing guinea pigs for roasting.

These costumed dancers are taking part in a parade in Venezuela, held to mark the Catholic feast of Corpus Christi.